D0991264

GIVE THE DOG A BONE

GIVE THE DOG A BONE

DARCEY & NICOLA MILLBANK

HQ
An imprint of HarperCollins*Publishers* Ltd
1 London Bridge Street
London SE1 9GF

10 9 8 7 6 5 4 3 2 1

First published in Great Britain by HQ
An imprint of HarperCollins*Publishers* Ltd 2018

ISBN 978-0-00-824603-7

Design by Louise Leffler

Our policy is to use papers that are natural,
renewable and recyclable products and made from
wood grown in sustainable forests. The logging
and manufacturing processes conform to the legal
environmental regulations of the country of origin.
For more information visit: www.harpercollins.
co.uk/green

Printed and bound in China by RR Donnelly

For Darcey, the 'Little Squid'

Darcey

CONTENTS

INTRODUCTION

A warm and tail-wagging welcome to *Give the Dog a Bone!*

I'm a cookbook author and the proud owner (albeit sometimes not-so-proud owner) of a very loving and playful miniature dachshund named Darcey. I have always loved making treats for Darcey: from biscuits to jerky, birthday cupcakes to 'oh no, I've run out of kibble' impromptu dinners, I've become quite inventive over the years and while the prospect of making biscuits, treats and other food for your dog might seem both whimsical and daunting, I assure you, it's extremely easy and a satisfyingly fun thing to do.

Despite our best intentions to feed our dogs the best it's always difficult to know what exactly goes into their treats. We've all heard the stories of junk being added to bulk out dog food, or the dangers of chemically bleached cow hide bones and hidden nasties in dog treats, making it hard to monitor what our pets are eating. The best way to really do this is to make food and treats yourself at home.

I'm aware that some dogs, just like us humans, have a wheat or nut allergy and so this book includes a number of gluten-free and nut-free options. However, for those dogs who enjoy peanut butter as much as Darcey, I urge you to make your own peanut butter from scratch. It takes minutes and is incredibly simple to do. A lot of cheaper supermarket brands contain oil, salt and artificial sweeteners, most notably a product called xylitol, a sweetener that is extremely toxic to dogs. The best way to avoid any doubt is to make your own nut butters yourself – you can even help yourself to some homemade peanut butter on toast for breakfast; it's 100 per cent peanuts and tastes delicious. If your dog has a peanut allergy, you can use cashews instead; although too many cashews can cause tummy problems, they are fine in small doses as treats.

As part of a varied diet, incorporating the right 'human foods' into your dog's mealtimes can be extremely beneficial for their health, so I've included a chapter that caters to easy treats and dinners, using ingredients that you might well be cooking for yourself and have going spare. Meatballs are an obvious hit, while egg-fried-rice muffins have saved me on those days when I've run out of dog food. Cooking broccoli or cauliflower that is a day or two past its best is the perfect way to avoid any food wastage and can be stored in the freezer until needed to add a nutritious and tasty accompaniment to your dog's meal.

While some recipes might be more appropriate to certain dogs than others, none of these recipes are breed-specific and will on average make about 12 or more treats. This will obviously depend on the size and breed of your dog and, when making biscuits, the size of the cookie cutter you're using. For Darcey I use a small cookie cutter, which is a good treat size for a dachshund, meaning there are always a few biscuits left over from the dough mixture. I tend to freeze leftovers (many of the recipes are suitable for freezing – see instructions in the recipes). If you're feeding a larger dog you'll want to use a larger cookie cutter, so you won't have as many left over, but it's important to remember that nobody knows your dog better than you and you'll know better than anyone what is a good-size treat and how often they should be allowed it. As with every treat, remember to give them as part of a varied diet and don't overdo it or you'll end up with a roly-poly; I speak from experience, Darcey was at one point a 'sausage roll'!

Making homemade dog treats is not only fun and a fantastic treat for the dogs in your life, it's also a great way to keep children entertained. All of the biscuit recipes are simply a combination of ingredients that require hands in bowls (the more the better) and rolling out dough, providing entertainment for kids who like playing with play dough, but with the added bonus of being able to feed the family pet something that they made themselves. To make things really easy, most recipes use a mug (rather than scales) to measure ingredients; mine is 300ml.

Many of the biscuits and treats will also make fantastic gifts, layered into a mason jar and tied with a ribbon as a small present or stocking filler, perfect for any dog owner or pampered pooch.

So I hope you enjoy making treats and other doggie delights from *Give a Dog a Bone*. My aim is to inspire all dog lovers who want to give their pets healthy and nutritious treats to get into the kitchen with their dogs and the family to make some homemade goodies. With meat, vegetarian and gluten-free recipes, all made with 100 per cent natural ingredients and available to buy in your local supermarket, I hope that this book of natural, healthy and easy recipes gets a paws up. Tried by me and tested by Darcey, these are some of her and her pals' favourites that I hope will become a firm favourite in your home too.

Love Milly and Darcey

BISCUITS

PEANUT BUTTER, OAT & CHICKEN STOCK BONES

A firm favourite with Darcey and friends, but then again anything with peanut butter in it always is! You can store these in an airtight container for up to a week or pop any you don't need in the freezer for up to 3 months.

YOU WILL NEED

Bone-shaped cookie cutter (or a round one works just as well)

1 mug wholemeal flour, plus extra for dusting

1 mug rolled oats

2 tbsp homemade peanut butter (see page 44)

½ mug warm chicken stock

Makes 12+

1. Preheat the oven to 180°C/160°C Fan/Gas 4.

2. Combine all of the ingredients in a bowl and knead well to form a dough (add a little water if it seems a bit dry).

3. Turn out onto a floured surface, roll out to about 5mm thick.

4. Cut out shapes with a cookie cutter, place on a non-stick baking sheet and bake for 18–20 minutes until golden.

APPLE & CHEDDAR CRACKERS

A gluten-free biscuit for pups who suffer from a wheat allergy. If you can't access brown rice flour then white rice flour is just fine. These will keep in an airtight container for a week, or can be frozen for up to 3 months.

YOU WILL NEED

Cookie cutter

1 mug brown rice flour

½ mug grated apple

¼ mug grated Cheddar cheese

½ mug warm water

Makes 12+

1. Preheat the oven to 180°C/160°C Fan/Gas 4.

2. Combine all of the ingredients in a bowl and mix well.

3. Turn out onto a lightly floured surface and roll out to about 5mm thick.

4. Cut out using any shaped cookie cutter and place on a non-stick baking sheet. Bake for 15–20 minutes until golden.

PEANUT BUTTER & BANANA BISCUITS

A sweet and nutty treat that almost every dog will enjoy.
If your pup has a wheat allergy simply substitute the wholemeal
flour with brown rice flour. These will live quite happily in an
airtight container for up to a week. Any that you don't need can
go in the freezer for up to 3 months.

YOU WILL NEED

Cookie cutter

1 mug wholemeal flour

½ banana, mashed

2 tbsp homemade peanut
butter (see page 44)

¼ mug water, plus extra
if needed

Makes 12+

1. Preheat the oven to 180°C/160°C Fan/Gas 4.

2. Combine all the ingredients in a bowl, adding
a little more water if necessary to bind the mixture
together.

3. Turn out onto a floured surface and knead well.
Roll out the mixture to about 5mm thick.

4. Cut out shapes using a cookie cutter and place
on a non-stick baking sheet. Bake for 18–20 minutes
until golden.

PIZZA TREATS

A fun alternative to the run-of-the-mill dog biscuits,
these pizza treats are a tasty and gluten-free biscuit that look
like mini pizzas. Stick to mozzarella or Cheddar for the topping
and only add a small amount, it's a treat after all! You can
store these in an airtight container for up to a week
or freeze them for up to 3 months.

YOU WILL NEED

Round cookie cutter

1 mug brown rice flour

1 tbsp vegetable oil

½ mug warm water,
plus extra if needed

2 tbsp tomato purée,
loosened with 1 tbsp water

¼ mug grated mozzarella

Makes 12+

1. Preheat the oven to 180°C/160°C Fan/Gas 4.

2. Combine the brown rice flour, vegetable oil and
warm water in a bowl, adding a little more water if
necessary to make a smooth dough.

3. Turn out onto a floured surface and roll out to about
5mm thick. Using a round cookie cutter, cut the dough
into discs and slightly pat them down so they look a
little more rustic.

4. Place on a non-stick baking sheet and bake in the
oven for 10 minutes. Remove from the oven, spread
a little of the tomato purée over each one and sprinkle
with grated mozzarella. Return to the oven for another
10 minutes until golden brown and crispy.

SWEET POTATO & BACON BITES

Sweet potatoes are a great source of fibre for your pups and are good for their digestion. Cook up the crispy bacon yourselves (pre-cooked bacon in packets has lots of nasty preservatives in it) – a good excuse for the human to have a bacon sandwich! You can store these in an airtight container for up to a week or pop any you don't need in the freezer for up to 3 months.

YOU WILL NEED

1 mug mashed sweet potato

2 rashers of crispy bacon, chopped into small pieces

1 mug coconut flour

½ mug warm water

Makes 12+

1. Preheat the oven to 180°C/160°C Fan/Gas 4.

2. Mix all of the ingredients in a large bowl until well combined.

3. Take pieces of the dough and roll into walnut-sized balls, then flatten using the back of a fork.

4. Place on a non-stick baking sheet and bake for 15–20 minutes until soft and lightly golden.

GOAT'S CHEESE & BROCCOLI BALLS

A healthy but tasty treat! If your dog isn't wheat-sensitive then you can substitute the brown rice flour for wholemeal flour. Store these in an airtight container for up to a week or pop any you don't need in the freezer for up to 3 months.

YOU WILL NEED

1 mug brown rice flour

½ mug finely chopped broccoli florets

¼ mug crumbly goat's cheese

½ mug warm water

Makes 12+

1. Preheat the oven to 180°C/160°C Fan/Gas 4.

2. Mix all of the ingredients in a large bowl, kneading well to evenly distribute the broccoli and goat's cheese.

3. Once fully combined, roll the dough into 1cm balls and slightly squash them down.

4. Place on a non-stick baking sheet and bake for 15–20 minutes until soft and lightly golden brown.

RASPBERRY & BACON BISCOTTI

These treats are quite dense and crunchy, so if your dog likes to really get stuck into something then this is the perfect treat for them. You can store these in an airtight container for up to a week or pop any you don't need in the freezer for up to 3 months.

YOU WILL NEED

2 mugs brown rice flour

4 rashers of crispy bacon, chopped into small pieces

½ mug fresh raspberries

¾ mug milk

Makes 24

1. Preheat the oven to 200°C/180°C Fan/Gas 6.

2. Mix all of the ingredients in a large bowl until well combined.

3. Using your hands, split the dough in half and form each half into two logs, pushing them down slightly to create biscotti-shaped logs.

4. Bake for 10–15 minutes and then remove from the oven to cool for a few minutes. Slice the logs into biscotti, about 1cm thick, place them back on the baking sheet and return to the oven for a further 10–15 minutes until dried out. Allow to cool and fully harden.

APPLE & YOGHURT DIPPED BISCOTTI

Another lovely, dense and crunchy snack but this time dipped into melted yoghurt drops for an extra-tasty treat. You can store these in an airtight container for up to a week or pop any you don't need in the freezer for up to 3 months.

YOU WILL NEED

2 mugs brown rice flour

1 apple, grated

1 tsp ground cinnamon

½ mug milk

½ mug yoghurt drops (you can buy these at most pet stores in the treat section)

Makes 24

1. Preheat the oven to 200°C/180°C Fan/Gas 6.

2. Mix the brown rice flour, grated apple, cinnamon and milk in a large bowl until well combined.

3. Using your hands, split the dough in half and form each half into two logs, pushing them down slightly to create biscotti-shaped logs.

4. Bake for 10–15 minutes and then remove from the oven to cool for a few minutes. Slice the logs into biscotti, about 1cm thick, place back on the baking sheet and return to the oven for a further 10–15 minutes until dried out. Allow to cool and fully harden.

5. To make the icing, melt the yoghurt drops in a heatproof bowl in the microwave on 10-second bursts. Dip one half of each biscotti into the yoghurt. Place on a sheet of baking parchment and chill in the fridge until set.

CHEESE & PINEAPPLE STARS

The retro cheese and pineapple gets a makeover into tasty dog-friendly biscuits. Pineapple is a great source of vitamin C for dogs and fresh is always best; if you do go for the canned variety, make sure you buy pineapple in natural juice as sugar syrup isn't good for dogs. You can store these in an airtight container for up to a week or pop any you don't need in the freezer for up to 3 months.

YOU WILL NEED

Star-shaped cookie cutter (or use any shape you have)

1 mug brown rice flour, plus extra for dusting

½ mug grated Edam or mozzarella

½ mug fresh pineapple, very finely chopped

¼ mug warm water, plus extra if needed

Makes 12+

1. Preheat the oven to 180°C/160°C Fan/Gas 4.

2. Mix all of the ingredients in a large bowl and knead until fully combined.

3. Turn out onto a floured surface, roll to a thickness of 1cm and then cut out shapes with your cookie cutter.

4. Place on a non-stick baking sheet and bake for 15 minutes until lightly browned.

SWEET POTATO PRETZELS

A real showstopper. A regular biscuit dough, but shaped into pretzels.
Sweet potatoes are a great source of fibre for your pup; if they are
wheat intolerant, substitute brown rice flour for wholemeal. Store in
an airtight container for up to a week or freeze for up to 3 months.

YOU WILL NEED

1 medium sweet potato,
peeled and chopped into
cubes

1½ mugs wholemeal flour,
plus extra for dusting

¼ mug freshly grated
Parmesan or Cheddar cheese

1 egg, beaten

Milk, for brushing

Makes 20

1. Preheat the oven to 180°C/160°C Fan/Gas 4.

2. Cook the sweet potato in a pan of boiling water for
5–8 minutes, or until soft. Drain and allow to cool.

3. Pop the sweet potatoes into a food processor and
blend until smooth. Spoon into large bowl and add
the flour, grated cheese and egg. Beat well until fully
combined and a dough has formed.

4. Tip the dough out onto a lightly floured surface
and knead for a few minutes until smooth. Divide the
mixture into about 20 even portions and then roll each
one into a long thin sausage, about 20cm long. Take
one long piece and shape into a 'U'. Twist the two ends
together and fold them back down over the bottom
part of the 'U' to make the classic pretzel shape.

5. Pop them on a baking sheet lined with baking
parchment and brush with milk. Bake for 20–25
minutes until golden brown, then set aside to cool.

TREATS

VEGGIE JERKY 4 WAYS

SWEET POTATO CHEWS

A great source of fibre and, once dried out, a deliciously chewy treat that your dog can really get their teeth stuck into! These will last in an airtight container for up to a month.

YOU WILL NEED

2 sweet potatoes

2 tbsp coconut oil

1 tbsp ground cinnamon

1 tsp honey

Makes 12+

1. Preheat the oven to 120°C/100°C Fan/Gas ½.

2. Slice the sweet potatoes into thin discs and pop them into a bowl with the coconut oil, ground cinnamon and honey. Give them a good mix.

3. Place the sweet potato slices on a non-stick baking sheet in a single layer. Wedge a wooden spoon in the oven door, keeping it slightly ajar to let any excess moisture out, and bake for 2–3 hours (depending on thickness). They should be dried out but with still a little chewiness in the middle.

PAPAYA CHEWS

Super-easy to prepare and so delicious – even humans can eat this one! These will last in an airtight container for up to a month.

2 papayas

Makes 12+

1. Preheat the oven to 120°C/100°C Fan/Gas ½.

2. Slice the papaya in half and spoon out the seeds. Slice each half into thin strips and pop them on a non-stick baking sheet. Wedge a wooden spoon in the oven door, keeping it slightly ajar to let any excess moisture out, and bake for 2–3 hours, or until dried out and bendy. The thinner you slice them the quicker they'll dehydrate, so keep an eye on them.

PINEAPPLE & BASIL RINGS

A great source of vitamin C, pineapple is a firm favourite!
Do use fresh pineapple here as it's much easier to cut into thin
slices. Make this in big batches and you can chew on them too
– they're perfectly good for humans! These will last in an airtight
container for up to a month.

YOU WILL NEED

1 pineapple

1 tsp olive oil

Small handful of fresh basil,
chopped

Makes 12

1. Preheat the oven to 120°C/100°C Fan/Gas ½.

2. Peel and core the pineapple and slice into thin
rings. Pop them into a bowl with the olive oil and
basil and give them a good mix until combined.

3. Place the pineapple rings on a non-stick baking
sheet in a single layer. Put into the oven – wedge a
wooden spoon in the oven door to keep it slightly ajar
and let any excess moisture out. Bake for 2–3 hours,
or until dried out and bendy. The thinner you slice
them the quicker they'll dehydrate, so keep an eye
on them.

COURGETTE STICKS

A healthy jerky made of only courgettes. Keep an eye on these while you're dehydrating them, as depending on how thick you slice them, they may dry out more quickly. These will last in an airtight container for up to a month.

YOU WILL NEED

2 courgettes

1 tsp olive oil

Makes 12

1. Preheat the oven to 120°C/100°C Fan/Gas ½.

2. Slice the courgettes lengthways into six thin strips then pop them into a bowl with the olive oil. Give them a good mix to coat in the oil.

3. Place them on a non-stick baking sheet and put into the oven, wedging a wooden spoon in the oven door to keep it slightly ajar and let any excess moisture out. Bake for 1 hour, or until dried out.

FROZEN YOGHURT & BERRY BITES

A super-easy bite-size treat that's perfect for the summer months. These can stay in the freezer for up to 3 months.

YOU WILL NEED

Silicone ice-cube tray

¼ mug mixed berries, such as blueberries and strawberries

1 mug natural yoghurt

Makes 12+

1. Mash the berries slightly using a fork and then press them into the bottom of a silicone ice-cube tray.

2. Spoon the yoghurt over the top of the berries and freeze for 8 hours or overnight. Turn each one out as and when your dog wants a tasty treat!

RASPBERRY & BANANA GRANOLA BALLS

A tasty and chewy fruit treat for your dog that's perfect as a 'breakfast' treat. You can store these in an airtight container in the fridge for up to a week or pop any you don't need in the freezer for up to 3 months.

YOU WILL NEED

2 bananas, mashed

½ mug raspberries, chopped

1 tbsp honey

1 mug rolled oats

Makes 12

1. Preheat the oven to 180°C/160°C Fan/Gas 4 and line a baking tray with baking parchment.

2. Mix all of the ingredients in a large bowl until fully combined, adding a little water if needed to bind the ingredients together.

3. Use an ice-cream scoop to drop balls of the mixture onto the lined tray. Bake for 10–15 minutes until set; allow to cool fully.

STRAWBERRY & BANANA FROYO

A super-easy froyo recipe that can be made and stored
in the freezer for up to 3 months. Serve by the scoop
as a treat on warm days. Great for humans too!

YOU WILL NEED

1 mug natural yoghurt

1 banana, mashed

½ mug strawberries, mashed

Makes 1 small tub (500ml)

1. Mix everything together in a large bowl until fully combined.

2. Transfer to a freezerproof plastic container and freeze for 2 hours.

3. Remove from the freezer and use a fork to mix up the frozen yoghurt and break up the ice crystals. Pop back into the freezer and freeze for 8 hours or overnight.

FROZEN WATERMELON & MINT BITES

Watermelon is the perfect treat for when it's hot, as it's rehydrating and full of flavour that dogs love. Don't give them too many, though, this is a sweet treat! These will keep in the freezer for up to 3 months.

YOU WILL NEED

Silicone ice-cube trays

1 mug diced watermelon

1 mug coconut water

1 tbsp honey

A few sprigs of mint

Makes 24

1. Throw everything into a blender and blitz until smooth.

2. Transfer to a pouring jug and divide the mixture evenly into the ice-cube trays.

3. Freeze for 8 hours or overnight. Turn each one out as and when needed.

DOG-FRIENDLY
STRAWBERRY ICE CREAM

On those hot days what better way to beat the heat than to
share an ice cream that's delicious for both pups and humans.
This will quite happily live in the freezer for up to 3 months.

YOU WILL NEED

1 mug fresh strawberries

½ mug coconut butter

3 mugs natural yoghurt

Makes 1 small tub (500ml)

1. Add everything to a blender and blitz until smooth.

2. Transfer the mixture to a freezerproof container and
pop into the freezer. Take out after a couple of hours –
ice crystals should have started to form. Use a fork to
mix it up again and return to the freezer, this time for
up to 8 hours or overnight.

3. Scoop a single serving into your dog's bowl for
a summertime treat and pop the rest back in
the freezer.

OSCAR'S OAT, BANANA & CASHEW NUT BUTTER TRUFFLES

Oscar is one of Darcey's pals and these are his favourite treats!
Your pups will absolutely love these; they are easy to rustle up
and no baking required – easy-peasy. Store them in the fridge
for up to a week or keep in the freezer for up to 3 months –
just take out as and when you want them and defrost at room
temperature for about 1 hour.

YOU WILL NEED

1 banana, mashed

¼ mug homemade cashew nut
butter (see page 44)

¾ mug rolled oats

1 tsp ground cinnamon

1 tsp honey

½ mug desiccated coconut

Makes 8–10

1. Put everything except the desiccated coconut
into a bowl and mix until fully combined.

2. Scoop a tablespoon-sized piece of dough into
your hands and roll into a smooth ball.

3. Roll each ball in the desiccated coconut and put
onto a plate lined with baking parchment. Pop them
into the fridge for about 30 minutes to firm up.

CHICKEN JERKY

The best type of jerky! You don't have to freeze the chicken before slicing but it will make them easier to cut. These will store quite happily in an airtight container for up to a month.

YOU WILL NEED

2 chicken breasts

1 tbsp honey

Splash of lemon juice

Makes 8

1. Put the chicken breasts into the freezer for an hour to make them easier to slice.

2. Remove from the freezer and slice lengthways into thin strips. Pop into a bowl with the honey, lemon juice and a mug of water. Cover and marinate in the fridge for 1 hour.

3. Preheat the oven to 80°C/60°C Fan/Gas ¼.

4. Place the chicken strips on a non-stick baking sheet and place in the oven. Pop a wooden spoon into the oven door to keep it ajar and let any excess moisture out. Bake for 3–4 hours, or until dehydrated and slightly bendy.

HOMEMADE PEANUT & CASHEW NUT BUTTERS

This is an absolute must – it's so easy. Shop-bought peanut
butter can contain xylitol, an artificial sweetener that's very toxic
to dogs, so unless you can be absolutely sure you're getting an
organic variety with no added salt or sugar, I recommend making
your own. This way you know there are no nasties in it
and that it's just 100 per cent nuts.
Cashew butter is a big hit with the pups, too – if your dog isn't
keen on peanut butter then this works just as well in any recipe
that calls for peanut butter. It will quite happily store
in a sterilised jar for up to 3 weeks.

YOU WILL NEED

Food processor

2 mugs dry roasted peanuts
or raw cashew nuts

Makes 1 jar of each

1. First sterilise your jar and lid by running them
through a dishwasher cycle.

2. Pour the peanuts or cashew nuts into a food
processor and let it run for 4–5 minutes. They will
go from crumbs to a dry ball and then into a creamy
butter. Don't be alarmed if it doesn't look like nut
butter at this stage; once it's passed the crumb phase
it will turn silky and smooth – just keep with it!

3. Spoon out into your sterilised jar and it's ready
to use in all your recipes.

CREAM CHEESE DRIZZLE CINNAMON ROLLS

Now this really is a treat! There's a little more prep involved but they're actually quite easy to make. They'll keep quite happily in an airtight container for up to a week.

YOU WILL NEED

2 mugs wholemeal flour, plus extra for dusting

4 tsp ground cinnamon

½ mug milk

¼ mug coconut oil

1 egg, beaten

2 tsp honey

1 egg, beaten, for brushing

For the icing

2 tbsp cream cheese

Makes 24

1. Preheat the oven to 180°C/160°C Fan/Gas 4 and line a baking sheet with baking parchment.

2. Sift the flour into a bowl and stir in half the cinnamon. In a separate bowl, whisk the milk, coconut oil and egg together. Slowly add this mixture to the flour mix and mix well until fully combined.

3. Turn the dough out onto a floured surface and knead for a couple of minutes until it has come together. Roll out into a rectangle about 5mm thick, brush with the honey and sprinkle with the remaining cinnamon. Roll the dough up and cut into 1cm slices.

4. Place the rolls on the lined baking sheet, brush with egg and bake for 15–20 minutes. Allow to cool fully.

5. Loosen the cream cheese with a little water until you have a drizzling consistency. Pour into a sandwich bag and snip off the corner. Drizzle the biscuits with the 'frosting' and allow to set fully in the fridge.

BANANA CHIPS

A healthy and tasty sweet treat that humans can enjoy too!
You can keep these in an airtight container for up to 3 weeks.

YOU WILL NEED

2 bananas

Makes 12+

1. Preheat the oven to 80°C/60°C Fan/Gas ¼ and line a baking sheet with baking parchment.

2. Slice the bananas and arrange the slices on the lined baking sheet. Pop the tray into the hot oven and slot a wooden spoon into the oven door to keep it ajar and let any excess moisture out. Bake for 3 hours, or until dehydrated.

MEALS

TURKEY MEATBALLS

A great savoury treat that's perfect at teatime. Serve as meatballs
or chop one up into your dog's food for some added goodness.
Once cooled these will keep in the fridge for up to 5 days –
the uncooked meatballs can also be frozen for up to 3 months.

YOU WILL NEED

2 mugs (about 500g) turkey
mince

1 mug cooked brown rice

1 carrot, grated

1 egg

Makes 24

1. Preheat the oven to 180°C/160°C Fan/Gas 4.

2. In a bowl mix the turkey meat for a couple of
minutes, then add the brown rice and grated carrot
and break in the egg. Mix well.

3. Roll the mixture into 24 meatballs about the size
of a walnut (at this stage I usually freeze half of the
meatballs for another time). Put the meatballs on
to a non-stick baking tray and cook for 25–30 minutes
until browned. Allow to cool before serving.

BAKED BROCCOLI & CAULIFLOWER

A delicious and healthy addition to your dog's meal that's low in calories. Give sparingly, however, as too much broccoli or cauliflower can cause stomach problems. This is the kind of side dish I make for myself and before I season it I give some to Darcey. This will keep in the fridge for a couple of days; alternatively, freeze the cooled broccoli and cauliflower and defrost in small batches as and when you need it.

YOU WILL NEED

½ head of broccoli

½ head of cauliflower

1 tsp coconut oil

1 tsp finely chopped parsley

Makes 4 servings

1. Preheat the oven to 180°C/160°C Fan/Gas 4.

2. Break the broccoli and cauliflower into florets, making sure they're all a similar size and pop into a bowl.

3. If your coconut oil is solid, melt it for a few seconds in the microwave, then pour over the cauliflower and broccoli. Scatter over the parsley and tip out on a non-stick baking tray.

4. Bake for 15–20 minutes until tender and the edges start to brown. Allow to cool before serving.

KALE, CARROT & PARMESAN MINI OMELETTES

A breakfast fit for both dogs and humans! Eggs are a great source of protein for dogs and if yours is suffering from a poorly tummy these can help. Go light on the Parmesan if that's the case but otherwise these make a delicious breakfast, best eaten the same day.

YOU WILL NEED

Silicone 6-hole muffin tray

6 eggs, beaten

¼ mug milk

¼ mug freshly grated Parmesan cheese

⅓ mug finely chopped kale

1 carrot, grated

Makes 6

1. Preheat the oven to 180°C/160°C Fan/Gas 4.

2. Mix all the ingredients together in a bowl and pour evenly into the holes of a 6-hole muffin tray.

3. Bake in the oven for 15 minutes until puffed up and set. Allow to cool before serving.

SHREDDED CHICKEN RICE BOWL

With lots of protein, healthy carbohydrates and vegetables this is a fantastic way to use up your Sunday roast leftovers. Sesame seeds in small doses are absolutely fine for dogs and actually contain antioxidants and omega-6 fatty acids. Adjust the portion to how much or little you feed your dog – you can store half in the fridge for up to 5 days or double the quantities if you have a bigger dog.

YOU WILL NEED

1 tsp coconut oil

½ mug cooked shredded chicken

½ mug cooked brown rice

¼ mug frozen peas

¼ mug grated cucumber

½ tsp sesame seeds

Makes 1 serving

1. Place a non-stick pan over a medium heat. Add the coconut oil to the pan, tip in the chicken and fry until it starts to brown.

2. Add the rice and peas and continue to cook for a couple of minutes until warmed through. Take the pan off the heat and add the grated cucumber. Stir to combine and allow to cool.

3. Scatter with sesame seeds before serving.

MOLLIE'S BEEF & EGG 'MUTTLOAF'

A real treat at mealtimes, Mollie's 'Muttloaf' is a delicious alternative to dinner on a special occasion! Once cooked, this will keep covered in the fridge for up to 5 days. Alternatively, slice into portions and freeze for up to 3 months.

YOU WILL NEED

450g loaf tin

2 mugs (about 500g) beef mince

1 egg, beaten

¼ mug chopped green beans

¼ mug grated carrot

2 tsp chopped parsley

4 hard-boiled eggs

Makes 1 loaf

1. Preheat the oven to 180°C/160°C Fan/Gas 4 and grease a 450g loaf tin.

2. Mix the beef mince, egg, green beans, grated carrot and parsley in a large bowl until fully combined. Divide the mixture in half, and press half into the bottom of the loaf tin.

3. Peel the hard-boiled eggs and lay them over the layer of mince, then cover them with the remaining mince, making sure it curves in and around the eggs.

4. Bake in the oven for 45–50 minutes, checking halfway through cooking and pouring out any excess moisture from the tin; it needs to remain dry.

5. Cool in the tin for 5 minutes before turning out onto a wire rack to cool fully. Serve by the slice as you would a loaf of bread; a 1cm-thick slice is a good portion for a medium-sized dog.

CHICKEN 'EGG FRIED RICE' MUFFINS

Another great leftovers recipe, but this time in the form of muffins. Great for breakfast or dinner, served as they are or chopped and added to your dog's regular food. These will keep in an airtight container in the fridge for up to 3 days.

YOU WILL NEED

Silicone 6-hole muffin tray

1 mug cooked shredded chicken

1 mug cooked brown rice

½ mug chopped broccoli

¼ mug frozen peas

3 eggs

Makes 6

1. Preheat the oven to 180°C/160°C Fan/Gas 4.

2. In a bowl, mix together the shredded chicken, brown rice, chopped broccoli and frozen peas. Crack in the eggs and mix fully to combine.

3. Spoon the mixture into a 6-hole muffin tray and bake in the oven for 15–20 minutes until set. Allow to cool before serving.

CELEBRATIONS

MEATLOAF & MASH 'PUPCAKES'

A meatloaf and mash combo that looks like a cupcake?
Absolutely! A lovely dish to whip up as a very special treat.
These will keep in the fridge for a few days, or you can freeze
the meatloaf part for up to 3 months and 'ice' when needed.

YOU WILL NEED

6-hole cupcake or muffin tray
lined with paper cases

2 mugs (about 500g) beef
mince

1 egg, beaten

¼ mug grated carrot

2 tsp chopped fresh parsley

4 medium potatoes, peeled
and cut into chunks

Splash of milk

¼ mug freshly grated
Parmesan cheese

Makes 6

1. Preheat the oven to 180°C/160°C Fan/Gas 4.

2. Mix together the beef mince, egg, grated carrot
and parsley in a large bowl until fully combined.

3. Spoon the mixture into the paper cases and bake
in the oven for 20–25 minutes. Transfer to a wire rack
to cool fully.

4. Meanwhile, cook the potatoes in a large pan of
boiling water for 8–10 minutes, or until soft; drain
and then use a potato masher to mash until smooth.
Add a splash of milk and the Parmesan and stir until
smooth. Allow to cool.

5. Transfer the mashed potato to a sandwich bag,
then snip one corner off and squeeze through the
hole to pipe the mashed potato over the pupcake
base to create 'frosting'.

BLUEBERRY YOGHURT ICED DOUGHNUTS

A very pretty treat, packed with antioxidant blueberries
that look like doughnuts! Keep these in an airtight container
in the fridge for up to 5 days.

YOU WILL NEED

Silicone 6-hole doughnut pan

1 mug wholemeal flour

1 mug milk

½ mug fresh blueberries

1 egg, beaten

½ mug yoghurt drops (you
can buy these at most pet
stores in the treat section)

Makes 6

1. Preheat the oven to 180°C/160°C Fan/Gas 4.

2. Put the flour, milk, blueberries and egg into
a bowl and mix well to combine.

3. Spoon the mixture into the holes of the doughnut
pan and bake in the oven for 15–20 minutes until
golden brown. Transfer to a wire rack to cool fully
before icing.

4. To make the icing, melt the yoghurt drops in a
heatproof bowl on 10-second bursts in the microwave.
Dip one half of each doughnut into the yoghurt, then
place on a wire rack and chill in the fridge until set.

APPLE & CINNAMON DOUGHNUTS

A delicious 'doughnut' recipe for those pups who are sensitive to wheat. If your dog isn't, simply substitute the brown rice flour with wholemeal flour. These will keep in an airtight container in the fridge for up to 5 days.

YOU WILL NEED

Silicone 6-hole doughnut pan

1 mug brown rice flour

1 mug milk

1 apple, grated

1 egg, beaten

1 tsp ground cinnamon

Makes 6

1. Preheat the oven to 180°C/160°C Fan/Gas 4.

2. Combine all of the ingredients in a large bowl and then spoon the mixture evenly into the holes of your doughnut pan.

3. Bake for 15–20 minutes until golden brown. Transfer to a wire rack to cool fully before giving to your dog.

PEANUT BUTTER & BANANA MINI CUPCAKES

These miniature cupcakes not only look lovely but are the perfect bite-size treat.

YOU WILL NEED

12-hole mini cupcake tray lined with paper cases

1 mug wholemeal flour

¼ mug rolled oats

1 tsp baking powder

½ mug mashed banana (about 2 bananas)

2 eggs, beaten

For the icing

½ mug water

4 tbsp low-fat cream cheese, chilled

2 tbsp homemade peanut butter (see page 44)

24 mini treats of choice, such as banana chips (see page 46)

Makes 24

1. Preheat the oven to 180°C/160°C Fan/Gas 4.

2. Mix together the flour, oats and baking powder in a large bowl. Add the mashed banana and eggs and stir until fully combined.

3. Spoon half the mixture into the paper cases until they are three-quarters full. Bake in the oven for 8–10 minutes, or until golden brown. Transfer to a wire rack to cool fully, then re-line the tray with paper cases and repeat with the remaining cupcake mixture to make a second batch.

4. For the icing, use a wooden spoon to beat the chilled cream cheese and peanut butter together and add enough of the water to make a pipeable consistency. Spoon into a sandwich bag, then snip one corner off and squeeze through the hole in the bag to ice the cakes any way you choose. Top with a small treat of choice.

VIKTOR'S STRAWBERRIES & CREAM VALENTINE KISSES

Viktor is Darcey's best friend in the entire world – she loves it when he comes over. These are for him. Keep in the fridge for up to 5 days.

YOU WILL NEED

12-hole mini cupcake tray lined with paper cases

1 mug brown rice flour

½ tsp baking powder

2 bananas, mashed

1 egg, beaten

2 tbsp honey

½ mug warm water

For the icing

4 tbsp low-fat cream cheese, chilled

1 banana, mashed

6 strawberries, hulled and halved

Makes 12

1. Preheat the oven to 180°C/160°C Fan/Gas 4.

2. Combine the brown rice flour and baking powder in a large bowl. In another smaller bowl mix together the mashed banana, egg, honey and water. Slowly add this mixture to the flour and baking powder and stir well until fully combined.

3. Spoon the mixture into the paper cases until they are three-quarters full. Bake for 8–10 minutes, or until golden. Transfer to a wire rack to cool fully.

4. For the icing, mix the cream cheese and banana together until smooth. Spoon the mixture into a sandwich bag, snip one corner off and pipe the icing over the cupcake bases. Top each one with a strawberry half on its end to look like a heart.

FROZEN PEANUT BUTTER & JELLY POPSICLES

A fantastic treat for those summer days. You'll need ice lolly moulds for this recipe and a few stick treats to act as the handle. Darcey loves chicken-wrapped hide sticks but a beef pissle or meat stick would work just as well. These will live quite happily in the freezer for up to 3 months.

YOU WILL NEED

6 plastic lolly moulds

4 mashed bananas

2 tbsp homemade peanut butter (see page 44)

10 strawberries, puréed

6 favourite stick treats

Makes 4

1. In a bowl, combine the mashed bananas and peanut butter until smooth. Add a little water to loosen – you're looking for a thick pouring consistency.

2. Pour half of the mixture into the base of the moulds. Freeze for 1 hour, or until set. Pour the puréed strawberries over the banana and peanut butter layer and pop back into the freezer for another hour.

3. Finally add the remaining half of the banana and peanut butter mixture into the mould. Pop a stick treat into the mould and press down into the first set layer. This should keep it upright but if it doesn't, secure with two rubber bands or pieces of sticky tape either side of the stick to keep it in place.

4. Freeze overnight to set fully. To remove from the mould, dip into warm water and carefully pull to remove.

BOOSTER
BITES

COCONUT OIL & CASHEW PAWS

A tasty treat and supplement for healthy skin and fur. If you don't already give your dog coconut oil you'll need to work up to the recommended daily allowance. Consult your vet or look on the internet to find out about recommended doses. These will keep in the freezer for up to 5 months.

YOU WILL NEED

Paw-shaped silicone mould (or an ice-cube tray will work just as well)

½ mug homemade cashew nut butter (see page 44)

3 tsp coconut oil, melted

Makes 12

1. Loosen the cashew nut butter with a little water in a bowl.

2. Half-fill the moulds with the cashew nut butter and freeze for half an hour. Once set, top each cube with ¼ teaspoon of coconut oil. Freeze again for 1 hour.

3. Top the moulds with the remaining cashew nut butter and freeze overnight.

PARSLEY & MINT PAWS

Let's be honest, as much as we love them sometimes we don't love their doggy BREATH! So you'll thank me for this one. These tasty parsley and peppermint paws will help with the problem. If you don't have a paw-shaped silicone mould just use an ice-cube tray. These will live happily for a couple of weeks in the fridge.

YOU WILL NEED

Paw-shaped silicone mould (or an ice-cube tray will work just as well)

½ mug finely chopped fresh parsley

¼ mug finely chopped fresh mint

½ mug coconut oil

Makes 12

1. Mix the herbs into the coconut oil. If it's not liquid just heat gently in a pan over a low heat until melted.

2. Pour the mix into your moulds and chill in the fridge overnight. Take out the mould when you need to and give one to your pup once a day until their breath is fresher!

GLUCOSAMINE & PUMPKIN PAWS

Glucosamine is great for dogs' joints and bones if they're feeling a bit stiff – you can buy it in most pet stores. Consult your vet or look online to find out the recommended daily dose for your dog's size. These will keep well in the freezer for up to 3 months.

YOU WILL NEED

Paw-shaped silicone mould (or an ice-cube tray will work just as well)

1 banana

¼ mug tinned pumpkin purée

Liquid glucosamine (see above)

Makes 6

1. Mix all the ingredients together in a blender and blitz until smooth.

2. Pour into your mould and then freeze overnight. Give one a day to your dog to combat stiffness.

FLAXSEED, BLUEBERRY & SPINACH SMILES

These smiles contain flaxseed, which is great if your dog suffers from the occasional bout of itchy skin. Store in the freezer for up to 3 months.

YOU WILL NEED

Smiley-face silicone mould (or an ice-cube tray will work just as well)

1 banana

¼ mug blueberries

¼ mug fresh spinach

1 tsp flaxseed

Makes 8–12

1. Put all the ingredients into a blender and blitz until smooth.

2. Pour into your mould and freeze overnight. Give one a day to your dog to soothe and heal itchy skin.

INDEX

ACKNOWLEDGEMENTS

Thank you to Lisa, Rachel, Louise, Sarah and the team at HQ, HarperCollins for seamlessly putting this book together.

To Ellis, for a wonderful photoshoot and for suggesting Darcey have an agent – what a FAB idea. And a big thank you to his fur-baby Frank for standing in for Darcey on the day.

Thank you to Michael and Richard, as always.

Thanks also to friends and family who have willingly given up their dogs for recipe testing.

And finally, to the Little Squid, Darcey, who's the best friend I could ever have wished for.